GREATER
VANCOUVER

JOSEF HANUS

Personal gift to :

From :

Captain G. Vancouver

A determined sailor, Captain George Vancouver of England became the first European to enter into the virgin waters of this area and named this channel 'Burrard Channel.' It was the night on June 12, 1792 that Captain Vancouver first anchored his ship near the shore of what today is Port Moody. He left the channel next day, June 13, to continue his search for the legendary Northwest Passage. Captain Vancouver was born in England's busy seaport, Norfolk's King's Lynn in 1757 and was appointed to the ship as a sailor at the age of fourteen. He sailed the seas for twenty years and in 1790 was promoted to commander, where he started the voyage of discovery that would lead him to the Northwest Coast. Captain Vancouver died at Petersham in 1798, at the age of forty. A monument in his memory has been placed in the park beside the Vancouver City Hall on Cambie Street, (pg. 24–25) where his statue stands, facing the city which was honored by his name 120 years ago.

History of Vancouver

1791– J.M. Navarrez, the Spanish navigator, arrived in the area but failed to reach the inlet. 1792–George Vancouver, English Captain, explored and named the inner harbour. 1808–Simon Fraser, fur trader and explorer, reached the Georgia Straight via the Fraser River. 1827–The Hudson Bay Co. set up the first fur-trade post in the area in Fort Langley. 1858–Thirty thousand prospectors arrive in the area, after gold was discovered in the Fraser River. 1859–New Westminster was named the capital city of British Columbia. 1867–Gastown opened the first saloon (pg. 6–7.) 1869–Granville becomes the second name for the young town. Gastown opens a jailhouse. 1886–Vancouver becomes the third and final name of the city on April 6. Two months later, the Great Fire destroyed more than 100 city buildings in just one hour. 1887–The first passenger train, Canadian Pacific Railway, arrives in Vancouver. 1902–The city population reaches 30,000 residents. 1904–The first train of the Great Northern Railway arrives in Vancouver. 1908–University of British Columbia was founded. 1929–The population reaches 250,000 residents and Vancouver becomes the third largest city in Canada. 1986–Expo'86 takes place in Vancouver. 2000–The population of Greater Vancouver reaches 1.6 million residents.

3

Burrard Inlet–North

The northern part of the Burrard Inlet, touching the shores of West Vancouver, Kitsilano, Stanley Park, Vancouver's West End and Point Grey, is an ocean playground for Vancouverites and tourists. One part of the Burrard Inlet, English Bay, is a popular recreational area. Recreational boats, moored at numerous ports, can be seen around many beautiful beaches all year round. Ships and tankers at sunset on Burrard Inlet are waiting to be loaded or unloaded. Burrard Inlet is one of the busiest commercial shipping ports in the world and welcomes over 3,000 ships from all over the world each year. Two centuries ago, when Captain George Vancouver entered the waters of this area and named it 'Burrard Channel,' there stood nothing more than tree-lined cliffs, pristine forest, and several native villages.

The First Builders

Just a century ago, the land around Burrard Inlet was a tangled coastal rain forest of colossal firs and cedars. As the loggers cleared the trees, the dense, damp woods gave way to a muddy landscape studded with giant stumps. Into this forbidding scene came Vancouver's first builders. Visionaries and dreamers, they were determined to create a proud coastal city out of this haphazard logging town. The coming of the railway in the year of Vancouver's incorporation in 1886, spurred a heady real estate boom and the construction of fine stone buildings for banks, hotels and commercial blocks. Large developers like the Canadian Pacific Railway and the Dominion Trust Company financed much of the construction, but many tiny companies headed by men rich from gold in the Klondike also threw in their lot. Among the most prolific of Vancouver's early architects was the partnership of Parr and Fee, who designed many of early Vancouver's buildings such as the Hotel Europe, the Vancouver Block and the Manhattan Apartments. W.T. Whiteway gave Vancouver The Landing, the Sun Tower and the original headquarters of Vancouver Fire department, the present day Firehall Arts Centre. W.M. Maclure was the finest of the residential architects, building many of the city's mansions, including the West End's Gabriola.

Water Street

The romance of golden ages surrounds you as you walk along Water Street in the oldest part of the city. Inviting restaurants and souvenir stores are set in this historical area, and the flowers decorate Water Street, accenting the vibrant brick architecture of yesteryear. The old city of Vancouver is typical of North American culture at the turn of the century. The older commercial buildings with their trademark fire escapes are the last reminders of golden days gone by. Pioneers first settled the area, building homes for their families and businesses. One of the first companies established in this area was Dominion Construction. The Dominion Trust Building, erected in 1909, became the first modern skyscraper in Vancouver, and was built near the Court House. Vancouver's first department store was opened by Charles Woodward in 1902, with its trademark red 'W' turning high above the city. Another curiosity is the Gastown Steam Clock, located in the centre of Water Street, built in England by Gilled & Johnston of Croydon.

6

Gastown

Gastown is the oldest section of Vancouver. The name was derived from a character named 'Gassy Jack,' alias John Deighton, who built the first saloon near Hastings Mills by Burrard Inlet. His saloon was very popular among the nearby workers and they built their houses near the area which later became Gastown. The area was registered as a community in March 1877, and named Granville after a British Colonel General's son. Today, Gastown is a famous tourist site. Water Street is the centre of Gastown, and is lined with souvenir stores, restaurants and historic houses and architecture. The Gassy Jack statue stands proudly on a whiskey barrel, his first market product after opening his saloon. The saloon was constructed in 24 hours with help from numerous thirsty employees of nearby Hastings Mills, where liquor was prohibited. Also in Gastown is Maple Tree Square, home to pioneer Canadian architecture, such as the Europe Hotel, designed in Victorian style by architect Thomas Fee.

Coal Harbour

Coal Harbour is a part of Burrard Inlet located between Stanley Park and the downtown core of Vancouver. Coal was discovered in this area by the British, hence the name Coal Harbour at the entrance to Stanley Park. Viewpoints from this area include Deadman's Island, The Vancouver Rowing Club and the white sails of Canada Place (see pg 9). The Vancouver Rowing Club, located in Stanley Park, was originally built in 1917, and still boasts one of the best views of downtown Vancouver. There are numerous gardens and small parks along the shores of Coal Harbour and on into Stanley Park, where one can stroll along the 10km seawall promenade, which took 60 years to complete. This famous and tranquil area is a popular spot for local residents and tourists alike who spend weekends visiting the Stanley Park Aquarium, Native Totem Pole display, or simply walking or biking through the area. Park your car in one of the large parking lots located in the Park, and trade your mode of transportation for a more romantic venue, such as a horse drawn carriage, a harbour cruise on one of the Harbour Ferries or on the historic vessel, the Constitution.

Canada Place

Canada Place is the most famous point in Burrard Inlet and in its original state was a cargo pier for large sea vessels. Canada Place was constructed for Expo'86 and became Vancouver's Trade & Convention Centre as well as the exposition site for the Canadian Pavilion. Canada Place is also home to fabulous hotels, the Pan Pacific and the Waterfront Centre Hotel. The modern architecture of the new hotels has turned Canada Place into an attractive business and tourist centre. Stroll the decks of Canada Place and view the magnificent cruise ships and vessels docking within the harbour. Visitors can be dazzled in the Imax Theatre, which features movies on a huge screen with special effects such as 3D. There are fine souvenir stores, and many fine restaurants to choose from, where one can enjoy a meal and a view from the table overlooking beautiful Burrard Inlet and the North Shore beckoning on the other side of the water. Canada Place was built over a three year period, and opened in May of 1986. The prow of the building is roofed by five graceful white sails, made from teflon coated fiberglass, which dramatically contrast the blue sky above.

9

Hastings Street

When the downtown core moved west from Gastown in the boom years before World War I, Hastings Street was developed as the new commercial centre of the city. Banks, offices, saloons and stores like the original Woodward's Department Store, built in 1908, sprang up along Hastings. Victory Square at Hastings and Cambie was the town's unofficial civic centre, and the site of Vancouver's first courthouse, built in 1888. Across the street was built the tallest building in the British Empire, the distinctive red-topped Dominion Trust Building. Erected in 1910, it was the first modern office building in the city, counting 13 floors. Two years later this building was eclipsed by the World Tower Building, just blocks away. The World Tower Building was raised 17 stories over the city and capped with a copper dome. Both buildings still stand today as a part of Vancouver's heritage. At the opposite end of Hastings Street, near Burrard, is another beautiful landmark of the city's architectural past, the Marine Building. Built in 1929, the Marine Building remains one of the finest examples of art deco in Canada. Here, elaborately bordered brass doors open into a lobby filled with richly decorated terra cotta panels depicting the Vancouver's modern history of exploration and transportation.

New Architecture

In the last twenty years, downtown Vancouver has experienced unprecedented growth, as massive developments like Robson Square, Canada Place, Pacific Place and the new Vancouver Public Library continue to change the face of the city. With a soaring real estate market and geographically restricted area, modern builders must seek creative ways to develop every useful square inch of land. Some companies such as the Canadian Pacific Railway's powerful Marathon Realty, represent continuity with the city's first builders. Most, however, are new companies headed by genius architects like Arthur Erickson, Paul Merrick, Richard Henriquez and Bing Thom. Vancouverite Arthur Erickson is considered among the most brilliant of Canada's architects, and the most pioneering of modern architecture since the 1950s. His work in Downtown Vancouver includes the massive Robson Square development containing the Law Courts and the Vancouver Art Gallery. Paul Merrick's vision is responsible for the Canadian Broadcasting Corporation offices, the renovation of the historic Marine Building and the Cathedral Place complex. Richard Henriquez gave the city the tastefully remodeled heritage buildings, making up the elegant Sinclair Centre. Bing Thom has brought modern architecture to historic Yaletown.

Vancouver Library

Vancouver Public Library is located on West Georgia Street, close to Queen Elizabeth Theatre and the Canada Post Building. This modern architectural wonder by architect Moshe Safdie and Associates, and Downs Archambault and Partners, was built by PLC Constructors Pacific Ltd. The construction, started in 1993 was finished in 1996. The library building has nine floors, of which 32,236 square meters are occupied by the library. On its shelves are housed 1.2 million items (books, periodicals and audiovisuals). The library is visited by 7,000 visitors daily. Besides books and magazines, the library collects art, music, maps and historical photographs. The business section provides a lot of good information and offers an extensive directory of different businesses around the world. Using the computerized data system, visitors can find telephone numbers and addresses for almost anyone on earth. Located on the Lower Level is the Children's Library. Gift shops and small restaurants offer souvenirs and refreshments to library visitors.

West Georgia Street

In 1887, the mighty Canadian Pacific Railway built the first Hotel Vancouver at the corner of Georgia and Granville streets, pulling the heart of Vancouver west from the old city of Gastown. Since then, Georgia Street has developed steadily as the business centre of downtown Vancouver. Today, soaring office towers gleam along this urban corridor. Because of its long-standing importance in the city, Georgia Street focuses many examples of modern and historic buildings along its route. The present Hotel Vancouver is the third such hotel built by the Canadian Pacific Railway. Finished in 1939, it is a traditional chateau-style railway hotel and retains much of its grandeur and elegance. Built in the 1880s, Christ Church Cathedral stands as the oldest surviving church in Vancouver. Overshadowing the little sandstone church is the impressive modern office complex of Cathedral Place. Developed in 1990, it has reinvigorated Georgia Street with shops, the Cathedral Square Park and the Canadian Craft Museum. The Hong Kong Bank of Canada is another contemporary office building with equally striking features. Inside its glassy exterior is an awesome public art installation. Mounted from the ceiling is a giant 28 metre, 1,590 kilogram buffed aluminum pendulum tracing a six metre arc back and forth across the bank's atrium.

Expo'86 Site

First occupied by the Canadian Pacific Railway's False Creek rail yards and roundhouse in 1986, the land on False Creek's north shore became the site of Vancouver's Expo'86 World Fair a century later. For the months of Expo celebrations, hundreds of pavilions and installations from countries all over the world turned this former industrial land into a daily party of crowds and colour. At the close of the fair, the land was sold to a private developer and today, Pacific Place, the largest private development is under way. Eventually housing for more than 10,000 people will be built here. Today, only a few reminders of Expo'86 remain. A familiar sight in the night sky is the twinkling geodesic dome housing Vancouver's Science World. Originally built as the Expo Pavilion, the dome contains the Omnimax Theatre, the largest domed theatre in the world. The pillowy, white structure of B.C. Place Stadium is another familiar landmark on Vancouver's skyline. The 60,000 seat Stadium was opened in 1983.

City Skyline

Vancouver…this beautiful city on the shores of the Pacific Ocean, the third largest city in Canada, is rapidly growing. 120 ago—at the end of 1886—Vancouver was a city of 5,000, looking confidently to the future. Today, Greater Vancouver is a city of 1.6 million people. A hundred photographs cannot capture this city, to display all its beautiful sights, culture, and attractions. This book was completed from about 240 photographs, carefully selected to display the most important parts of Vancouver, its downtown, beaches and parks, and all the interesting places around Greater Vancouver. The photographs on this page show the city skyline from three different positions. Above, from the North Shore across the Burrard Inlet. At right, from West Broadway. At bottom, downtown from Spanish Banks Beach,

Night in the City

As the sun sinks its last fading rays into the ocean behind the dusty blue slopes of the Howe Sound Crest Mountains, night settles over the city. A necklace of twinkling, jewelled lights traces the outline of the mountain peaks at the ski areas of Grouse Mountain and Cypress Bowl. On the surrounding ocean, the glow from boats and buildings streak the dark waters with silver fingers of light. Down in the city, locals like to say that Vancouver wakes at the sound of Stanley Park's Nine O'clock Gun. The neon lights of a rich diversity of restaurants, bars and clubs illuminate the streets as urban dwellers leave work behind for a night on the town. On the beaches, lovers sit on logs gazing to the sea, long after the sun has disappeared. On Robson Street the crowds promenade, seeing and being seen. On Granville Street the theatres fill up, while those in the mood for live entertainment line up for rock bands at the 1930's era Commodore Ballroom, or for the symphony at the historic Orpheum Theatre. For those who enjoy nightlife of any kind, Vancouver hosts a cosmopolitan world within a relatively small city.

Downtown

Vancouver is a city on the rise, with a downtown core ever changing into a more cosmopolitan and international urban centre. Despite the growing pains of big city density and traffic, Downtown Vancouver remains a friendly, easy place to explore. The downtown's outward growth is contained by its near island-like setting. Set on a narrow peninsula, it seems one could hold the urban core in the palm of one's hand. Crossing from end to end takes no more than an hour. Encircled on all sides by water, the streets remain open and light. Invariably, a glimpse down any corridor of skyscrapers reveals a refreshing scene of mountains and water. The modern day business centre of Downtown Vancouver is the result of a century old power struggle between east and west; between the old interests of the Gastown elite and the emergent interests of the mighty Canadian Pacific Railway (CPR.) When Vancouver was incorporated in 1886, Gastown was the heart of the city. Just a year later however, the CPR began aggressively developing their land west of the city centre, at present day Granville and Georgia. Ultimately, the CPR triumphed, and one hundred years later, the downtown core is still centered to the west, where Granville and Georgia intersect.

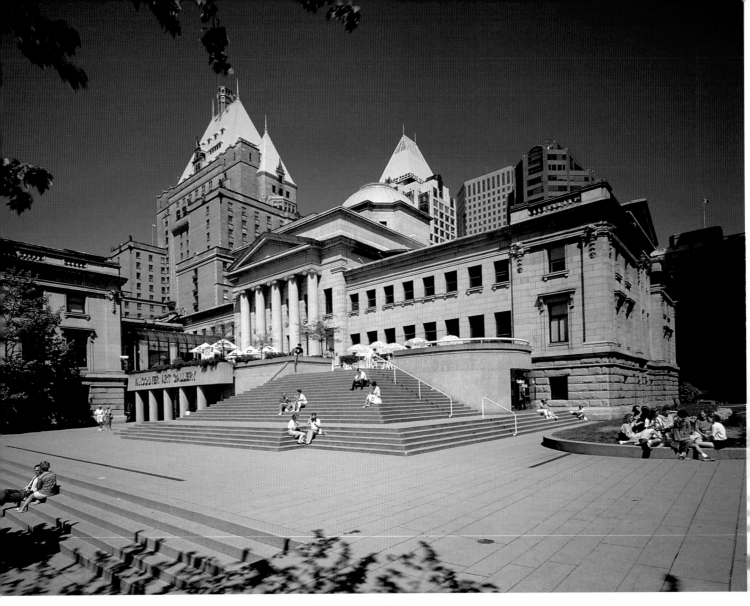

Robson Square

Running from downtown Vancouver through the West End, Robson Street is a bright, bustling mecca for shoppers. Originally the commercial centre of the German community, the street was called Robsonstrasse, and the nickname has held. Through the 1980's Robson Street was reinvented, developing the city's most fashionable urban scene. Small, fashionable boutiques both sophisticated and contemporary crowd corner to corner along the street selling a wide variety of designer clothing, gifts, housewares and books. Sandwiched between the many shops are a host of trendy coffee bars and restaurants, offering some of the best food the city has to offer. Robson Street is the pulse of downtown Vancouver. By day shoppers jostle from store to store, and cafés overflow with the lunch crowd. On summer nights shops are open late and the streets are busy with couples enjoying an evening promenade and colourful people on their way out for dinner. The Vancouver Art Gallery stretches from Robson Street to Georgia Street and has become a cultural and civic focal point. Originally Vancouver's courthouse, the building was redesigned in 1979 by Arthur Erickson. The back steps of the gallery on Robson Street have become an unofficial speaker's corner and meeting place for friends and political rallies alike.

Granville Island

For half a century, Granville Island, nestled under the Granville Bridge, was a dank, crowded industrial park producing things like rivets, nails, cement and chain-link in its noisy factory warehouses. Today, Granville Island has been transformed. Though the cavernous corrugated metal warehouses and the atmosphere of industry remain, Granville Island is now a hub of colour and creativity, producing things like pottery, plays, children's toys and chocolates. Now, at Granville Island visitors can charter a boat, see a play, dine by the sea, buy local crafts, meet artists and shop for dinner. The heart of Granville Island is the Granville Island Public Market, where specialty foods, fresh from the farm or the oven, overflow from every stall. Outside in the court-yard, crowds enjoy lunch on their laps, entertained by performers from the Bluegrass, Folk, Jazz and Comedy Festivals. A separate spectacle unfolds on the waters below, as boats of every description pass in and out of False Creek. Across the rest of Granville Island, ware-houses have been reborn as a variety of modern urban spaces. A walk through Granville Island will reveal three theatres, a host of fine restaurants and bars, and more than 30 studios and galleries showcasing the work of local artists and craftspeople.

19

Burrard Street, Bridge

The westernmost of the crossings spanning False Creek, Burrard Street and bridge are a vital link between the urban core and Vancouver's westside neighbourhoods. Even pedestrians enjoy the bridge, which affords a sweeping uninterrupted view west across English Bay toward the waters of the Strait of Georgia. On the sparkling waters below, bright sailboats dot the bay and busy ferries spirit passengers back and forth between English Bay, Granville Island and the Maritime Museum. The building of a bridge across English Bay and Burrard Street was first suggested in the Harland Bartholomew Town Plan of 1927, which was prepared in anticipation of the amalgamation of Vancouver with Point Grey and South Vancouver. Construction began on the piers and supports of the bridge in 1930, and the Burrard Street Bridge was finally opened on Canada Day, 1932. Designed by engineer Major. J.R. Grant, the modern six lane bridge was built well above the shipping lanes below. The massive steel superstructure was camouflaged under the direction of the Public Art Commission, with a concrete portal in the spanish colonial art deco style of the day. On Burrard Street are several hotels and St. Paul's Hospital. Wall Centre, Burrard Street's newest addition, is now the tallest Vancouver building. (Photo on pg. 11).

Granville Street, Bridge

The Granville Bridge, a vital link to Downtown Vancouver from the south, was among the city's very earliest bridges. Built to improve access to the Fraser River from Downtown Vancouver, the Granville Street Traffic Bridge was opened by Mayor David Oppenheimer in 1889. At a cost of $16,000, the bridge was just wide enough for two wagons. Barely clearing high tide, it was so low that boys would fish and swim off of it in the summers. Twenty years later, this original low level timber trestle was replaced by medium level steel bridge with a swing span for marine traffic. The Governor General of Canada, Earl Grey and his wife Lady Grey, opened the new bridge in 1909. The second Granville Bridge was a spur to the development of Kitsilano and Shaughnessy, providing commuters with a convenient route downtown. Eventually, however, with the inexorable rise of automobile traffic through the 1940's and 50's, the swing-span proved an impossible inconvenience. The present day Granville Bridge was opened in 1954. It follows the alignment of the original bridge, but has eight lanes and is a fixed span built well above False Creek and Granville Island.

21

Aerial View

The city of Vancouver occupies one of the most stunning settings in the world, inviting comparisons to Hong Kong, Cape Town, and San Francisco. Sheer snow capped mountains rise dramatically out of the perfect natural harbour. The urban core is contained on a broad peninsula, surrounded on all sides by the shimmering waters of the Pacific Ocean. Stunning views of the city can be enjoyed from lookout points and from the mountains. A favorite place to look over all of Vancouver's areas including Stanley Park, Vancouver International Airport, Richmond, the whole of Burrard Inlet and Vancouver Island, is from the Cypress Bowl Road, high above West Vancouver. The photographs on this page were taken from an airplane.

False Creek

The waters under the the Granville Bridge were first surveyed by Captain G.H. Richards of the Royal Navy. While exploring the environs of Burrard Inlet, he mistook the waters here for a stream running into English Bay, and thus marked the narrow inlet of False Creek. Though some have attempted to replace this appellation with one more lyrical, the name False Creek has stuck. The land around False Creek south to Broadway was developed as an exclusive residential neighbourhood by the Canadian Pacific Railway in 1890. The vista from the bluffs on the inlet's south earned the neighbourhood the name of Fairview. By the early decades of the century even a fair view could not compensate for the foul odours that began to rise from False Creek's rapidly developing sawmills, shipyards and factories. The area remained intensely industrial until the 1950's, when Broadway was redeveloped. Today, with its multitude of offices and services, the Broadway Corridor has become an important business district and Vancouver's second downtown. In the 1970's the industrial waterfront of False Creek was finally reclaimed. False Creek is now dotted by sailboats and encircled by a lovely pedestrian seawall. On the hillside above is a bright patchwork of condominiums and parks, housing a new urban community.

Cambie Street, Bridge

Cambie Street is the first main street of Vancouver's westside, and is one of Vancouver's major thorough-fares, slicing through the heart of the city to the eastern edge of the downtown core. Cambie is a lively commercial street, and a popular place to live. To the south Cambie crests the highest point in the city, Little Mountain, the site of Queen Elizabeth Park. Down at the sea level is the Cambie Street Bridge. The first bridge connecting Cambie Street to Downtown was a simple piled timber trestle with a trussed swing span built in 1891. In 1912, a second bridge was built with a wood and steel structure that still had to be opened 2 or 3 times a week for marine traffic. The newest Cambie Street Bridge was completely rebuilt for Vancouver's World's Fair, Expo '86, and is the most modern bridge in the city, with six lanes and a deck raised well over False Creek.

Vancouver City Hall

The area around Vancouver's City Hall is at once urban and peaceful, commercial and residential. The Broadway Corridor is a bustling commercial area, and to the south the sprawling buildings of Vancouver's General Hospital dominate. The hospital has grown considerably, since it opened in 1906 with 100 beds, as the city's first public, non denominational hospital. The surrounding neighbourhood boasts some of the finest and most beautifully maintained heritage houses in the city. The area's gentrification is reflected in the soaring glass and contemporary shops of City Square. Created from two fine stone heritage buildings, City Square reveals stunning contrasts of old and new. Vancouver City Hall was not built until 1935, after nearly a decade of debate over its site. Under the firm hand of the city's most colorful and dynamic leader, Mayor Gerry McGeer, the corner of 12th and Cambie was chosen, as it straddled east and west and offered a fittingly panoramic view over the city below. Despite the hardship of the Great Depression, Mayor McGeer managed to raise the million dollars needed to complete the stark, modernistic building by selling baby bonds. City Hall was opened in 1936 as part of Vancouver's Diamond Jubilee celebrations. More than half century later, the building remains a proud city landmark.

Parks and Gardens

Queen Elizabeth Park, in addition to being the most famous garden park in Vancouver, also has the highest elevation at 150 metres. The name was established after the royal visit of King George IV and Queen Elizabeth in May 1939. This garden paradise is frequented not only by tourists and photographers, but is also a popular site for weddings among the locals. On any given Saturday from April to October. you can expect to see up to 4 or 5 wedding parties at the same time! The 52 hectare garden has a pitch-and-putt golf course, 20 tennis courts, and rose and tropical gardens, which are habitat for hundreds of tropical birds who fly freely in the plexiglass dome of the Bloedel Floral Conservatory. Smaller in size but just as beautiful, is the Vandusen Botanical Garden (22 hectares,) home to 6,500 different kinds of plants gathered from six continents. A favorite site for children is the Elizabethan maze, planted with towering cedars. This garden was opened to the public in August 1975. Other popular viewing gardens include Dr. Sun Yat-Sen Chinese Garden, the botanical gardens at the University of British Columbia, Park & Tilford Gardens, Nitobe Memorial Garden...over 200 gardens in all can be found in Greater Vancouver!

Mount Pleasant

Mount Pleasant is a part of Vancouver located south of
False Creek, between Cambie Street and Main Street.
Mount Pleasant began life as Vancouver's first suburb,
and was simply known as 'across the creek,' until it was
aggressively developed in the 1880's. Today, this neighbourhood is again experiencing redevelopment and
renewal. The eastside of Main Street has cultivated a
brisk antique trade and a lively art scene, annually host-
ing the Fringe Festival Theatre event. These photographs
of the Mount Pleasant area, including False Creek, were
taken from the highest building on West Broadway.

Vancouver Museum

Steel Crab, dominating the entrance of the Vancouver Museum, is a visible landmark of Kitsilano. Canada's largest civic museum has served as the keeper and interpreter of Vancouver's heritage for more than 100 years. A walk through the museum is a walk through the history of the surrounding region. Since its opening nearly a century ago, the museum has continued to collect amazing artifacts from around the world in its spectacular 'Orientation Gallery,' and tours the city's early beginnings in the 'Exploration and Settlement of Vancouver.' The Vancouver Museum is committed to the education of people and is Vancouver's premier venue for national and international exhibitions. A first-hand perusal of Vancouver's history can be obtained next door at the Vancouver Archives, which contain thousands of historical photographs and documents. Rising out of the park like a massive space ship is the HR. MacMillan Planetarium. Under the landmark white conical roof is a rotating Zeiss projector, which with over 130 projectors and 50 different lenses, recreating the stunning sights of the universe on a dome-like overhead screen. The Virtual Voyages full-motion flight simulator launches you on pulse-pounding missions across the galaxy. Standing in the shadow of the planetarium is the Gordon M. Southam Observatory.

Vanier Park

Vanier Park, at the foot of English Bay, is a breezy, rolling, manicured field favoured by joggers and kite flyers. A wide, gravel seaside path winds around the towering West End. Just offshore, the historic boats of Heritage Harbour are floating marine museums. Nearby in the neighbourhood, located on the beach is the Vancouver Maritime Museum, showcasing Canada's marine heritage. Centre stage here is a national heritage sight, the St. Roche. Built for the Royal Canadian Mounted Police in 1928, this schooner became the first ship ever to circumnavigate North America, in 1950.

Lions Gate Bridge

Towering two hundred feet above the First Narrows of Burrard Inlet stands Vancouver's trademark bridge, named after the nearby Lions Peaks. Completed in 1938, the bridge was financed by the Guinness Family and constructed by Pratley and Monserrat engineers. Mayor L. Taylor wanted a four lane bridge, but the Guinness investment of 6 million dollars was enough only for a three lane bridge. Eastern Canadian financiers were not willing to invest any more for the fourth lane. The bridge, 6,000 feet long, is an important link between Vancouver and the North Shore. Deep in the water underneath the Lions Gate Bridge, resting on the harbour water's floor, lays the first steamship to arrive on the Pacific Coast—the S.S. Beaver. This famous ship was launched by the Hudson's Bay Company in England in 1835, and was shipwrecked on the rocks of Prospect Point in 1888, where it still remains. Some pieces of the S.S. Beaver are displayed in Vancouver's Maritime Museum (see pg. 29–Vanier Park).

English Bay

English Bay is the broad sweep of water stretching west of the Burrard Bridge and lapping up against the shores of Point Grey, Kitsilano, and the West End. More specifically, however, English Bay refers to the sandy crescent tracing the waterfront from the Burrard Bridge to Stanley Park, in the shadow of the West End high rises. The name commemorates the chance meeting in 1792, between British Captain George Vancouver and the great Spanish explorers Don Dionisio Alcala-Galiano and Don Cayetano Valdes. Since that historic encounter some two hundreds years ago, English Bay has become the recreational hub of Vancouver, giving the city its best beaches, sailing waters and sunset strolls. Today, English Bay is one of Vancouver's oldest attractions, drawing flocks of bathers as early as the 1890s when the West End was first developed. Countless West End children learned to swim here during the early years of the century under the unfailing care and instructions of Vancouver's most celebrated lifeguard, Joe Forest. English Bay continues to entice hordes of summer swimmers, sunbathers and windsurfers into the chilly waters offshore. Even in winter the brave and the foolhardy splash into the frigid bay, during the annual Polar Bear Swim on January 1st.

31

West End

West End is Vancouver's most urban neighbourhood. Within the jungle of apartment buildings that give the city its distinctive skyline is Canada's most densely populated square kilometre, stretching west from Burrard Street. Within its boundaries are the main streets of Denman, Davie, Robson, Burrard and Georgia. When first developed by the Canadian Pacific Railway in 1886, the West End housed Vancouver's earliest elite in luxurious estates far from the noisy city. In the crowded patchwork of the modern day West End, very little of the neighbourhood's posh beginnings remain. The most opulent of the old mansions, Gabriola, once the center-piece of an expansive estate, today houses a restaurant on busy Davie Street. The Roedde House Museum, in a historic house at Barclay Heritage Square Park, offer a taste of the West End's era of Victorian elegance. Despite its high density, the modern West End remains a friendly and livable neighbourhood. Surrounded by the ocean and park, and broken up by small residential streets, it does not feel cramped or overrun with traffic. Pedestrians enjoy peaceful strolls by the sea, or along tree lined streets. Neighbours shop, gather and enjoy the view in the many popular cafés, boutiques and galleries that line Denman, Robson, Thurlow and Davie streets.

Kitsilano

When the Canadian Pacific Railway first put land in Kitsilano up for sale in the early years of the century, no one was very interested. Today Kitsilano, which derives its name from a revered local Squamish chief, is among the most popular neighbourhoods in Vancouver. Home to hippies in the 1960's, Kitsilano is now more favoured by condo-dwelling young professionals. Many streets are still lined with colourful heritage houses from the 1910's and 1920's. With their wide front porches and overhanging eaves, they lend the neighbourhood an old fashioned charm. Skirted by oceanfront parks, sandy beaches and seaside paths, Kitsilano is the consummate west coast community. Along the busy commercial streets of 4th Avenue and Broadway, lovely shops, cafés and restaurants overflow with customers. At Kits Beach, swarms of glistening sunbathers crowd towel to towel across the hot sand throughout the long days of summer. Families enjoy picnics, the playground and the heated 137 metre long (150 yard) Kitsilano Pool. Offshore the white coloured triangles of the sailboats and windsurfers from the Kitsilano Yacht Club glint in the sun.

Point Grey

Captain George Vancouver named this part of Burrard Inlet after his friend and fellow sailor Captain Grey. The components of a beautiful, natural setting—numerous beaches and parks, captivating views of downtown, North Shore mountains, and English Bay have made this area a highly desirable place to call home. The commercial centre of Point Grey is the intersection of Alma Street and 10th Avenue. In Pioneer Park stands Vancouver's oldest building, the 'Hastings Mill Store,' one of the few survivors of the Great Fire of 1886. Spanish names like Langara Street, Blanca Street, Locarno and Spanish Banks were named after Spanish sailors, the members of Commander Navarrez' crew, who landed here in 1792. Locarno Beach was once one of three original B.C. native villages—the other two being originally located in Stanley Park and near Capilano River in North Vancouver. Pacific Spirit Park, the largest park on Point Grey, offers 800 hectares of forest and beaches, with 50 km of trails, from the shores of English Bay to the north areas of the Fraser River.

Jericho Beaches

Spanish Banks, Jericho, and Kitsilano Beaches are spread along the shores of English Bay from Kitsilano to Point Grey. The beaches are favored resting and sunbathing places for Vancouverites. The waters are warmed by the sun drenched sand, heated during low tide, attracting people who play in the shallow waters. Stony beaches are points of interest for numerous photographers and painters, waiting here for the last moments of the day, when the very low sun creates warm scenic images. The above photograph of a rocky beach with a stormy downtown Vancouver was shot just a second before sunset on the beach by Tatlow Park.

Universities

Founded in 1908 and built on the tip of beautiful Point Grey, the University of British Columbia is now the biggest university in the province, educating more than 45,000 students. The centre of campus life at UBC is the Main Library. Other offerings at UBC include the world's largest cyclotron, the Asian Centre, the Frederic Wood Theatre and the Museum of Anthropology. Lovely beaches, parks and gardens are favourite places for relaxing or studying for students and visitors alike. In 1926 the UBC Botanical Garden was founded here. Covering 47 hectares, the flora of China, the Himalayas and Japan can be discovered at the David. C. Lam Asian Garden. The Simon Fraser University, perched atop Burnaby Mountain, was opened in 1965. Designed by eminent architect Arthur Erickson, SFU is a fine example of modern architecture, meeting the needs of several tens of thousands of students and fitting beautifully into its natural surroundings. it is not uncommon to find a deer feeding on the grass in between parking lots on campus. Viewpoints on Burnaby Mountain are the best way to glimpse the expanse of the City of Burnaby below, and Deep Cove to the north.

Wreck Beach

Large rocks in shallow water made a dangerous combination for many ships which sank here in long past days, inspiring the name 'Wreck Beach.' Today, this isolated beach with its unrivaled natural beauty, is one of a kind in the Lower Mainland. The beach, located near the University of British Columbia, offers an awesome view from the tip of Point Grey peninsula across the Strait of Georgia. In the early evening, enjoy the crashing ocean waves and scenic outline of Vancouver Island's mountains. The location of Wreck Beach is difficult to find, but well worth the trouble. A steep trail winds down to the beach from North West Marine Drive, near Cecil Park. High above Wreck Beach is the recently erected Museum of Anthropology and U.B.C. Nitobe Memorial and Botanic Gardens. Those willing to wait in Cecil Park for sunset will be delighted with the fantastic view of the silhouette of ships in the Pacific Ocean.

Stanley Park

With over 40 hectares of forest, beach, garden, park and trail, Stanley Park offers something for everyone all year round. Naturalists will enjoy close-up bird watching at Lost Lagoon. Hundreds of water birds and song birds alight at this bird sanctuary during migration. A walk on the seashore will provide a fascinating look at the colourful intertidal life of Vancouver's coast. The forest trails of the park offer a glimpse of Vancouver's ancient rainforest, where Douglas fir and western red cedar tower above the ferns on the dark floor. Inside the park, a host of attractions include the Miniature Train, the Rose Gardens, Prospect Point, the Hollow Tree, Siwash Rock, and the Teahouse Restaurant. The Stanley Park Seawall is a continuous marine promenade encircling the entire park. It is a favourite spot for joggers, cyclists and sunset strollers. For visitors it is a lovely way to tour Stanley Park. This spectacular ocean path represents 60 years of human endeavor. Beginning in 1917, hundreds of labourers toiled over the 10.5km snaking seaside structure until its completion in 1980. Today the seawall reveals breathtaking views of Vancouver's surroundings, including Burrard Inlet and English Bay.

Vancouver Aquarium

With 8,000 animals representing 600 species, the Vancouver Aquarium is a wonderland of aquatic discovery. From Arctic Canada to the Amazon rainforest, the aquarium provides a fascinating glimpse of the colourful and vital life beneath the world's waters. A private non-profit institution, the Vancouver Aquarium was founded in 1950 with a mission to conserve and enhance aquatic life through education, recreation and research. Today it is one of Vancouver's top attractions, faithfully supported by over 55,000 members and thousands of daily visitors. The most popular inhabitants of the Vancouver Aquarium are the distinctive black and white Killer Whales, who occupy the main pool with the dolphins. Some 400 wild Killer Whales live in the ocean near British Columbia, making the whale population of this coast the largest in the world. The captive whales at the aquarium have greatly increased our understanding of the rich spirit and intelligence of this magnificent species. Other highlights at the aquarium include the H.R. MacMillan Tropical Gallery, the Graham Amazon Gallery and, for a closer look at the marine life, just offshore, the Sandwell North Pacific Gallery.

Totem Poles

In 1890, a plan was born to recreate a West Coast native village at Brockton Point. The village never materialized, but several artifacts including a collection of totem poles, a native war canoe and the petroglyph rock were installed. The assembled totems stand today next to a lush grove of mixed deciduous and evergreen trees. They are dramatic reflections of the rich culture that existed in this region before the coming of the Europeans. Totem poles are carved from western red cedar, and are vulnerable to the ravages of the elements. The collection of poles at Brockton Point have therefore changed over the years. The various peoples represented, include the Kwakiutl, Haida, Nisgaa and Nuu-chah-nulth. Totem poles are not religious icons, rather they serve to tell a personal story of a family history and have various ceremonial functions. The poles at Brockton Point include a house post, a memorial pole and a mortuary pole. Some of the figures commonly carved are animals such as Bear, Wolf, Raven, Eagle, Frog, Killer Whale and Hawk. Mythical beings also have their place on the totem poles. With thunder rolling from its wings and lightning flashing from its eyes, the Thunderbird is considered the mightiest of supernatural spirits and can only be adopted as a crest by the most high-ranking of people.

Siwash Rock

When Captain George Vancouver first sailed into Burrard Inlet, he believed Stanley Park was an island. In fact, the massive promontory is a part of the mainland mushrooming out into Burrard Inlet. For hundreds of years before the arrival of the Europeans, the Squamish people used the land here as a seasonal camping ground. At present day Lumberman's Arch, a giant midden filled with their ancient debris remains undisturbed under the ground. It is thought to extend for an area of 1.8 hectares and to be as deep as 2.5 metres. When the British laid claim to the coast, today's peaceful park was set aside as a military reserve. This promontory at the head of the inlet was seen as a protective bulwark against a possible American incursion. The grand civic park enjoyed so much by harried city dwellers and visitors alike, was proposed at the first meeting of Vancouver's first city council meeting in 1886. In 1889, Canada's Governor General Lord Stanley publicly dedicated his namesake "to the use and enjoyment of people of all colours, creeds and customs for all time." More than a century later, Stanley Park remains a delight through every season of the year.

Harbour and Ports

Vancouver's Harbour is a busy port that hums with the constant movement of marine traffic. Cruise ships sidle up to the Pan Pacific Hotel, sea planes arrive and depart, tug boats weave their busy paths back and forth, and huge tankers from far flung lands move silently into port. In November 1864, the departure of the Australia-bound ship 'Ellen Lewis' marked the birth of international shipping from Vancouver. Since that first lumber shipment, Vancouver's port has become Canada's largest. It is also one of the top three foreign-tonnage ports in North America, linked with over 90 countries worldwide. Visitors can enjoy a closer look at Vancouver's port from several spots around the city, including the Public Viewing Centre at the Port of Vancouver's Vanterm. Canada Place offers a sweeping view of surrounding industry, with information plaques mounted around its promenade. Parks perched on the harbour, including Portside Park, Harbour View Park and of course, Stanley Park.

The Lions

The Coast Mountains form a dramatic backdrop to the city of Vancouver, stretching from Howe Sound to Indian Arm, and reaching heights of over 1500 metres. They are a tremendous resource, offering an array of recreational pursuits from hiking to skiing. Even more importantly, the mountain watersheds fill the reservoir of Capilano Lake with clean, fresh drinking water for the entire city. Of these mountains, the most famous are the twin peaks standing high above the rest as silent sentinels over the world below. This jagged pair are known as 'The Lions,' named after the Landseer Lions in London's Trafalgar Square. Poet Pauline Johnson immortalized them in her book *Legends of Vancouver*: "You can see them as you look towards the north and the west, where the dream-hills swim into the sky amid their ever-drifting clouds of pearl and grey. They catch the earliest hint of sunrise and they hold the last colour of sunset." In her conversation with Squamish Chief Joe Capilano, she discovered, that native name for the same peaks was 'The Two Sisters.' According to legend they represent twin sisters immortalized in stone for their role in bringing two warring peoples together.

43

West Vancouver

With the mountains above and the ocean below, West Vancouver is a rugged haven prized by its dwellers. An historic failure to attract industry began a legacy of strict town planning that proved to be the municipality's saving grace. In 1931, encouraged by the stringent building codes, Britain's Guinness family purchased 1,620 hectares of land on Hollyburn Ridge to develop the exclusive residences of the British Properties. To enhance the value of their community, the family also financed the building of the Lions Gate Bridge and the Park Royal Shopping Centre. Today, large house lots, quiet streets and peaceful parks give West Vancouver an air of genteel island life. Dramatic modern homes speak of rich seclusion. The small shopping villages of Ambleside and Dundarave are filled with boutiques and restaurants that evoke sophisticated small town living, removed from the urban centre. Beginning under the Lions Gate Bridge is the Centennial Seawall Promenade. This lovely seaside path along West Vancouver's shore passes the grassy expanse and popular beach of Ambleside Park and ends a little farther along at Dundarave Beach. Every morning the whistle of Canada's only running steam locomotive can be heard as it passes through Ambleside Park on its daily trip up the coast to Squamish.

Horseshoe Bay

Nestled deep between the misty cliffs of the Coast Mountains on Vancouver's North Shore is Horseshoe Bay. Rising up sharply on all sides, the dark, forested rocky faces of rugged mountains are a dramatic surrounding for this tiny seaside community. From the protected waters of the bay, the British Columbia Ferries trace their continual path to Snug Cove on Bowen Island, just 20 minutes away, to Langdale on the Sunshine Coast, a 40 minute trip, and to Departure Bay on Vancouver Island, a 90 minutes crossing of the Strait of Georgia. For those who miss their ferries, Horseshoe Bay reveals a relaxing, friendly face with plenty to do to pass the time. A number of restaurants line the waterfront, offering a variety of seafood delicacies, from fish and chips to sushi. Centennial Park forms a grassy shoreline walk with shady maples forming a canopy over picnic tables and children's playground. At the park's eastern edge, Sewell's Marina juts into the bay, dotting the water with an assortment of fishing boats, pleasure cruises, and even floating houses. Some of the best salmon fishing spots in Vancouver are just offshore, and fishermen can be seen here, casting off into the promising waters. Photo at centre right is a view from Cypress Mountain, overlooking Horseshoe Bay.

Grouse Mountain

The peak of Vancouver and the centre of the row of mountains above Vancouver, Grouse Mountain is a part of the Coastal Mountains. Next to challenging skiing, this recreational area offers some of the best views of Greater Vancouver. Night skiing with a view of fluorescent downtown is a very popular activity. Grouse Mountain is the highest point above Greater Vancouver and can be reached very easily from downtown by public transit and the Skyride gondola. There is skiing terrain for everyone from experienced skiers to novice skiers searching out new adventures. Grouse Mountain is very popular, even during the summer months. Families with children will find picnic tables, lawns and playgrounds. More active visitors can hike around Blue Grouse Lake, or to other peaks nearby. Grouse Mountain's close neighbour to the northwest is Crown Mountain. The highest peak above Vancouver at 1501 metres (5000 ft), with a distinctive rocky formation called 'The Camel' next to its summit, Crown Mountain can be seen from most points around Greater Vancouver.

Burrard Inlet–South

The area of the south part of Burrard Inlet which can be seen from several view points around Stanley Park or from North Vancouver, unfolds in front of you like a fantastic aerial map. Beautiful cruise ships ply the Vancouver Harbour during summer months, as this picture shows. On a clear day, watching the whole area from Cypress Bowl Road viewpoint,—the best place to see the whole of Burrard Inlet—one can see Stanley Park, downtown Vancouver, and Vancouver's International Airport, located in Richmond. The mountains of Vancouver Island, the whole expanse of Greater Vancouver, and even the white glaciated peak of Mt. Baker in nearby Washington State are also visible. The first industry in this area was a sawmill, established on the north shore, now North Vancouver, in June, 1863. Today, much of British Columbia's industry is located around Burrard Inlet, as fishing industry, sawmills, fish canneries, storage facilities, wheat and sugar silos, and ship repair yards. Watching Burrard Inlet from the Second Narrows Bridge, this part of Greater Vancouver seems like a beehive of activity.

Portside Park

Beautiful Portside Park is located east of Canada Place, close to Gastown and Main Street. This small, peaceful park offers grassy slopes, stony beaches and children's play areas. This relatively quiet place is a good spot to watch the wildlife in Burrard Inlet. Nearby is the SeaBus Terminal, Heliport, Canada Place and numerous shipping docks and dry docks. Canada Place Promenade and the Seawalk will lead you around Coal Harbour to Stanley Park.

48

Capilano River and Bridge

Small but breathtaking is the privately run Capilano Suspension Bridge, occupying one corner of the 160 hectare Capilano River Regional Park. The original suspension bridge was suspended here in the 1880's by settler George Grant Mackay, and by Natives August Jack and Willie Khahtsahlano. Ever since, visitors have been making the trek up the Capilano River to cross the perilous canyon on the swinging bridge. Today, Capilano Road makes this trip somewhat easier, but the ancient canyon retains its craggy, misty, primeval wonder. Water streams over its cliffs, and crooked trees cling to its edges. The modern suspension cables are encased in tons of concrete, but the bridge still retains its rustic allure. Nothing but cedar planks separate those crossing from the rushing river 69 meters below. The rocky riverbed beneath is a daunting sight when glimpsed through gaps in the wood. Every step seems to set the bridge's 137 metres length swinging and rocking over the canyon. The surrounding public park offers many attractions, including Capilano Lake, the awesome Cleveland Dam and trails the length of the river, which passes many prime fishing spots. The Capilano Fish Hatchery provides a fascinating close-up look at the life cycle of the river's salmon and trout.

Lighthouse Park

On the rocky shores at the western edge of West Vancouver shines the beacon of the Point Atkinson lighthouse, a landmark of Vancouver's coastline for the last 80 years. The 75 hectares surrounding the lighthouse form Lighthouse Park, the city's most sanctified wilderness park. Here stands the last undisturbed remnant of the great rainforest that once covered every inch of the coast. It is an ecological snapshot of the city's ancient environs. The grey-green trunks of the Douglas fir tower overhead, reaching heights of up to 80 metres. Dark green Western hemlock and ruddy peeling western red cedar complete the canopy of the rainforest, soaked by more than 125 centimetres of rain every year. On the shady forest floor, sword ferns, salal, Oregon grape and salmon berries form a tangled undergrowth. The chatter of Douglas squirrels and the song of migrant wood warblers fill the fragrant humid air. Mossy granite boulders loom, gouged by volcanic intrusions, their ancient rock worn smooth at the water's edge. The rocky shore is a favourite spot for sunset picnics, with a constant parade of marine traffic and the blue inlets of the gulf glistening southwards.

Cypress Mountain

Perched above West Vancouver, on the wooded rise of Hollyburn Ridge and the rocky face of Black Mountain, Cypress Provincial Park is a beautiful mountain park with a multitude of recreational uses all year round. In the summer, hikers and casual walkers alike enjoy the network of trails that criss-cross through the park. Campsites, picnic tables, nature trails and swimming spots like Cabin Lake, increase the summertime opportunities at the park. When the snow begins to fall, the skiers and snowboarders take over the slopes. Boasting the greatest vertical drop of the North Shore mountains, Cypress provides some of the most challenging skiing the city has to offer. The best cross-country skiing in Vancouver is also found at Cypress with 27 kilometers (17 miles) of groomed trails weaving across the gentler slopes of Hollyburn Ridge. To enjoy what most consider the most spectacular feature of Cypress Provincial Park, one need not even leave one's car. Just minutes off the highway, a stunning roadside lookout reveals an expansive bird's eye view of the city from the west. Vancouver seems to float in Burrard Inlet, while Point Grey extends into the Strait of Georgia. In the distance, blue islands dot the gulf towards Vancouver Island.

Indian Arm, Belcarra

Belcarra, Deep Cove, and Indian Arm can be seen from the top of Burnaby Mountain Park. Washed by the waters of Indian Arm, the Belcarra Regional Park is in front of you, as if you could hold it in the palm of your hand. The multitude of waterfront picnic areas, and numerous campsites make it a favourite place for school children and hikers. A trip down Indian Arm, at 20 kilometres the longest part of Burrard Inlet, will let you explore the wild nature of the Mainland from the sea. The views of Mount Seymour Provincial Park and the wooded, craggy cliffs will make this an unforgettable trip. Deep Cove is one of the most beautiful spots in North Vancouver, scenically located at the foot of Seymour Mountain, on the shore of Indian Arm. This very quiet place with its sunny beaches is among the most desirable places both to live and visit. Clear deep water with little traffic offer excellent fishing, which can be enjoyed all year long.

Mount Seymour

Reaching up into the craggy peaks at the eastern edge of North Vancouver's rugged mountains is Mount Seymour Provincial Park. Here the heights are covered with a dense alpine forest, where amabylis and yellow cedar compete with the small, hardy mountain hemlock. Following its steep, winding 13 kilometre (8 mile) path up the mountain side, Mount Seymour Road enters the park's parking lot at an elevation of 1,037 metres (3,400 feet). Along the way are two breathtaking lookouts. The first allows a backdoor look at the shimmering city to the west. The second offers a glimpse east over Deep Cove and the winding fjord of Indian Arm. In the winter, the peaks here are popular with snowboarders and novice skiers. In the summer, Mount Seymour is a popular destination for hikers. The park is carefully laid out with a refreshing variety of hikes offering something for everyone. Hikes like the Dinkey Peak Trail and Mount Seymour Trail take hikers to the top of the North Shore mountains, with heady, magnificent views of surrounding peaks, the city below, and the Strait of Georgia beyond. Other, easier strolls are no less rewarding, leading walkers through subalpine meadows bright with flowers.

North Vancouver

Located on Vancouver's North Shore, east of the Lions Gate Bridge, North Vancouver is a study in contrast. Within its boundaries exist both a busy industrial site, and the quiet reaches of the mountain wilderness. Unlike neighbouring West Vancouver, North Vancouver has had no trouble attracting industry. Beginning in 1863, with the opening of Pioneer Mills, North Vancouver has remained a hub of industry. Today, North Vancouver's waterfront is a vital part of Vancouver's port, its docks handling grain, coal, sulphur and potash exports.

North Shore

A growing residential community, North Vancouver is ever expanding, with high rises crowding Marine drive, and subdivisions creeping up the mountains. It is a favourite for families wishing to live in the city, without paying exorbitant city prices. The redevelopment of historic Lower Lonsdale has revitalized North Vancouver's waterfront. The SeaBus, launched in 1977, is a delight for commuters harried by bridge traffic, bringing them home from downtown Vancouver in mere minutes. Adjoining the SeaBus terminal is the Lonsdale Quay Public Market. Opened in 1895, Lonsdale Quay is a bright, bustling marketplace, filled with fresh food stalls, shops, cafés and restaurants. Just offshore, busy tugboats pass by, and in the distance is a full view of Vancouver's urban landscape.

Shaughnessy, Arbutus

Between 16th Avenue and King Edward Boulevard, Vancouver's landscape rises in a steep climb above the city. Little Mountain near Cambie Street is the highest point in the city, at 150 meters above sea level, but all across Vancouver, the land reaches heights affording beautiful vistas of the city below. The land at 16th and Granville was developed by the Canadian Pacific Railway in 1907. Determined to create the most exclusive residential area west of Montreal's Mount Royal and north of San Francisco's Nob Hill, the CPR laid down the spacious boulevards and expansive house lots of Vancouver's most elegant neighbourhood, Shaughnessy. The atmosphere of Shaughnessy remains one of genteel affluence. Some of the historic homes of Vancouver's early rich, such as Highcroft House, Villa Russe and Glen Bare, still stand today evoking the grandeur of Old Shaughnessy. Further west along King Edward, the bluffs above Vancouver support the neighbourhoods of Kerrisdale, Arbutus, and Mackenzie Heights, where pretty homes enjoy views toward the Strait of Georgia. In the spring, the streets around King Edward erupt into a wonderland of cherry blossoms. Boulevards of blossoming cherry trees form archways of colour. Spiraling in the wind, the petals rain down white, pale pink and dark pink into the streets.

Kerrisdale, Langara

A favourite residential area located on Vancouver's south slopes, south of 41st Avenue, Kerrisdale, Langara, South Cambie and Killarney are known as the South Neighbourhoods. Numerous parks and golf courses located on the southern slopes offer rich opportunities for sport and recreational activity. A favourite destination for Vancouverites interested in a day of golfing, in numerous beautiful golf courses, is the area around Fraser River. Richmond and Vancouver International Airport can be seen from many points. Langara College is located by 49th Avenue and Ontario Street. Punjabi Market, well known as Little India, is located on Main Street between East 49th and 51st Avenue. An interesting point of Little India is a Sikh Temple, designed by Vancouver architect Arthur Erickson. Busy streets, South West, South East Marine Drive, and the North Arm of Fraser River border the Fraser River across from Richmond.

Theatres

Numerous theatres, concert halls and movie theatres in Greater Vancouver area offer fine performances for those who like the arts and music. Every month, music festivals at Granville Island, or on the shores of English Bay, such as the duMaurier International Jazz Festival or Vancouver Chamber Music Festival, attract tens of thousands of music lovers. Vancouver's most famous music institute, the Vancouver Symphony Orchestra, performs frequently at its home, Vancouver's gracious and elegant Orpheum Theatre. Hundreds of world renowned artists perform every year in Vancouver. BC Place Stadium is a great spot for the largest events—famous singers such as the Three Tenors, or operas like Aida, performed several years ago. Ballet BC and Royal Winnipeg Ballet perform downtown at the Queen Elizabeth Theatre, which is offers six full-scale productions each season, including classical, comedy, drama and musicals. The Vancouver Film Festival, which takes place in October, offers Vancouverites the best in current cinema from around the world. Vancouver's jazz artists also perform daily in numerous cafés.

Summer Beaches

The rains of winter are fast forgotten as the sun calls forth Vancouver's fantastic blossoms in April and May. Tourists and locals alike fill their free time at the beautiful sandy beaches all around the city. Vancouver boasts not only the most kilometres of sandy beaches for a large city within Canada, but also for any large city in North America. These lovely beaches abound in English Bay, with names like Jericho Beach, Wreck Beach, Spanish Banks, First, Second or Third Beach in Stanley Park; or Ambleside Park in West Vancouver, and Crescent Beach in Surrey and White Rock. But not only in summer months. In fact, the beach season starts on New Year's Day in English Bay with the annual Polar Bear Swim attracting 2,000 swimmers into the chilly waters and 20,000 spectators in warm coats to watch this event. But still the best life on Vancouver's beaches is in the summer, and there's no admission charged for any of the beaches!

Burnaby Village Museum

At the Burnaby Village Museum, visitors can step back in time with a little imagination, and witness the area encompassing this transition. Villagers costumed in period dress complete the picture of historic Burnaby at this living museum. They churn butter, dip candles and hammer iron, and run an antique printing press. A stroll down Main Street will reveal a host of shops and offices, including a bakery, pharmacy, general store, autoshop and optometrist. Even a dentist office stands, complete with all the fixtures of the 1920's. The Electric Theatre recaptures the spirit of the twenties with silent movies. Of special interest is 'Old Curly,' the oldest surviving steam locomotive in British Columbia. An even earlier mode of transportation, the horse drawn carriage is also a fixture at this living museum. Special events throughout the year highlight Christmas, Easter and Thanksgiving, but every day offers a chance to enjoy hands-on activities, displays, demonstrations, and entertainment from years past. A favorite event is the 'Canada Day' Celebration, when a huge cake, decorated with a Canadian Flag is offered to visitors.

Deer Lake Park

Surrounded by a beautiful park, Deer Lake is nestled near Canada Way in Burnaby. A full day can be easily spent in the park watching wildlife—mostly birds, or to try one's luck with the fishing rod, fishing for trout or carp. In the neighbourhood is the Burnaby Art Gallery, housed in Ceperly House Mansion. Burnaby Arts Centre and the popular James Cowan Theatre is also located close to Deer Lake. The park is located on Burnaby's north slopes, which have dramatically changed in the last ten years. Beautiful houses in this modern subdivision are home to thousands of residents enjoying life in the city, and in the park too. A well maintained trail through the park and around the lake is a special place favoured by joggers and walking residents. In summer months, visitors can rent a canoe or kayak and enjoy the view of surrounding shores from the water. The beach is a favourite place for children, playing in the sand, surrounded by hundreds of water birds, such as Canada Geese.

Burnaby Mountain

The suitably named 'Playground of the Gods' is one of the most popular parts of Burnaby and Burnaby Mountain Park. This place, decorated with numerous Totem Poles, is located close to Simon Fraser University. This beautiful park and playground is visited by thousands in summer and cherished for its snowy hills by children in winter. From its dramatic rise high above the city, a magnificent view is revealed of downtown Vancouver on one side, and Indian Arm, Deep Cove, Belcarra Regional Park, Port Moody and Coquitlam, on the other side. Neighbouring the 'Playground of the Gods' is the growing enclave of Simon Fraser University, opened in 1965. Burnaby Mountain is an excellent autumn destination for thousands of amateur photographers, shooting pictures from the viewpoint high above Indian Arm, or for those falling in love. Visitors can enjoy the shore of Burrard Inlet at Barnet Marine Park, or enjoy one of the finest views of the whole city.

Burnaby

Originally settled by loggers and farmers, Burnaby is now a thriving suburb. Just a short SkyTrain ride to downtown Vancouver, Burnaby is developing quickly to meet the housing demands of local commuters. At the same time, Burnaby boasts lively retail and business areas of its own. Central to Burnaby on the SkyTrain route is the giant Metrotown Mall, where shoppers can take advantage of over 375 shops and services. Simon Fraser University, opened in 1965 and boasting the modern architecture of Arthur Erickson, continues to draw students from all over Canada to its campus on Burnaby Mountain. Burnaby was incorporated as a municipality in 1892, and numbered 250 people as its citizens. By the 1920's, Burnaby was in transition from a rural area to the urban centre it is today. Despite the quick pace of development, however, Burnaby maintains its wild green spaces. The 750 acre Burnaby Lake Regional Park is the area's biggest public park, and is centered around Burnaby Lake. Deer Lake park offers a host of amenities, including the Burnaby Arts Centre with its theatre, art gallery, restaurant and formal gardens. The 222 acre Central Park has been a landmark in Burnaby since 1891, when the Central Park tramline was the hub of Vancouver's electric rail system.

New Westminster

In 1858, miners struck gold in the Fraser Valley. Within months, 20,000 gold seekers flooded through the Hudson's Bay Company's Fort Langley, threatening the peace in this formerly sleepy trading post. In short order, the British government named the area a British Colony and dispatched a corps of Royal Engineers to establish law and order. Headed by Colonel Richard Clement Moody, the engineers chose high ground next to the Fraser River, before the branching of its north and south arms, to build the capital city. Queen Victoria dubbed the settlement New Westminster and it remained British Columbia's capital until 1868, when it was superseded by the present day capital, Victoria. New Westminster is known as the 'Royal City' because of this exalted history. Visitors can gain an excellent introduction to New Westminster's colourful history with a visit to the Westminster Museum, and the Irving House Historic Centre. Irving House was built in 1864 by pioneer river-boat Captain William Irving, and preserves the atmosphere of 19th century life in the colonies. Today, New Westminster is a bustling town on the SkyTrain route, preserving heritage houses while developing modern urban amenities. The lively Westminster Quay Public Market is a bright waterfront farmer's market, surrounded by hotels, condominiums, and restaurants.

Fraser River

The Fraser River has always been an important traffic vein serving the West Coast. The Pattullo Bridge, railway, and SkyTrain Bridges can be seen high above the Fraser River, from New Westminster's embankment—a favourite place of weekend visitors to New Westminster's Quay Public Market. The Fraser River, springing from the Canadian Rockies, flows over 1,500 kilometres through British Columbia and empties into the Strait of Georgia around Richmond. The Fraser River is a waterway which brought into the Greater Vancouver area not only the first pioneers such as Simon Fraser, but gold prospectors, fur traders and more. The river's course formed during thousands of years, with alluvial deposits covering a huge area, today named the Fraser Valley.

Langley

The agricultural centre of Langley is well known as 'The Countryside of Vancouver'. Langley, with its major centers—Fort Langley, Aldergrove and Langley City (main photo) are located between Matsqui and Surrey. Fraser Highway is a major route connecting Langley, Surrey, Vancouver, Matsqui and Abbotsford. Numerous farms, located along highways grow vegetables. Locals like to stop at some farms or roadside vegetable stands to buy fresh farm products, or pick berries and fruits themselves, directly from orchards. There are several large shopping malls to serve the needs of the booming suburban communities, located by the Langley Bypass in Langley, where they are concentrated next to large car dealerships and numerous industries.

Fort Langley

Fort Langley is a picturesque pastoral town east of Vancouver, on the south shore of the Fraser River. Lovely cafés and a bountiful antique market line its pretty streets. Fort Langley is a town rich with history, offering a glimpse into the oldest European settlement in the Pacific Northwest. Fort Langley was established by the British Hudson's Bay Company in 1827 as an outpost, to strengthen its hold on the region's lucrative fur trade. When the British Government founded New Westminster as the capital of their far flung colony, the commercial importance of Fort Langley was eclipsed, and by the year of Vancouver's incorporation, 1886, Fort Langley was closed. Today, the rough hewn structure of Fort Langley is a National Historic Site, evoking the spirit of the frontier. Summer programs offer history lessons with films, demonstrations and many hands-on activities led by volunteers, costumed in pioneer dress. History buffs can travel even further back in time, at the Langley Centennial Museum and National Exhibition Centre. A fascinating display of native artifacts from the Coast Salish reflect the life of this land's very earliest dwellers. The collection includes a partial replica of a traditional house, wood and stone sculptures, baskets, and various tools.

Port Moody

East of the Second Narrows Bridge, the narrow, snaking Burrard Inlet splits into two branches. The north branch travels deep into the heart of Indian Arm. At the foot of the south branch lies Port Moody. The freezing of the Fraser River in 1859 gave life to Port Moody. With their water route to the salt water port of Burrard Inlet frozen, New Westminster's Royal Engineers realized the necessity of building an overland route. They built the North Road to the foot of Burrard Inlet and named the area Port Moody after their leader, Colonel Moody. In 1885, the settlement experienced a brief heady land boom when the Canadian Pacific Railway announced that the western terminus of their great national railway would be Port Moody. A frenzy of land speculation followed, but when the site of the terminus was moved to Vancouver, Port Moody was plunged into a prolonged depression. Port Moody developed as an industrial area with saw mills, wood processing plants, and the Ioco oil refinery. Despite the industry, Port Moody has the feel of a coastal small town where seals can be found, sunning themselves on the Inlet's log booms. Near Ioco's huge refinery is the secluded expanse of Belcarra Park, with its peaceful seaside paths and beaches. A popular summer destination for thousands is Buntzen Lake.

White Rock

Just minutes away from the American border, the village of White Rock is a sunny southerly suburb of Vancouver. With its small town feel and lack of rain, White Rock is a popular spot to live and visit. Despite its small size, White Rock is the most cosmopolitan of Vancouver's suburbs. Along with its mild coastal climate comes a distinctly Californian atmosphere with modern ocean-side houses clinging to cliffs, and a bustling promenade of beachside cafés. White Rock gets its name from the giant white boulder perched on its beach. According to legend, the rock was thrown across the Strait of Georgia by the son of a seagod. A visit to White Rock is a good way to get close to the sea. Semiahmoo Park, just south along White Rock's beach is a popular picnic spot. Even a short walk on the beach, or along the pier will reveal beautiful views to the south. Occasionally even a pod of migrating whales can be spotted. Artist Robert Wyland's mural 'Whaling Wall,' painted on a building in downtown White Rock, is a beautiful depiction of the majestic grey whales that migrate up and down the coast.

Surrey

A vast suburb south of the Fraser River, towards the American border, Surrey has held a reputation as the fastest growing community in all of Canada. Surrey has enjoyed tremendous booms in its town centers of Cloverdale, Whalley, Guildford, Newton and Sunnyside, thanks to the beautiful and affordable housing built by local architects. Despite the fast pace of development, Surrey does retain much of its rural charm. Farms line the highways and roadside vegetable stands brim with fresh produce all summer long. On the May long weekend, Surrey celebrates its country roots in cowboy style with the annual Cloverdale Rodeo. The second largest professional rodeo in Canada, and sixth largest in North America, the Cloverdale rodeo attracts the finest cowboys in the world to compete in bull riding, saddle bronco riding, steer wrestling, bareback riding and calf roping. The rodeo brings out crowds from across the continent with cheering audiences of over 7,000 attending. Cloverdale is also the site of much of Surrey's heritage, with many historic buildings. British Columbia's third largest community history museum, the Surrey Centennial Museum and Archives, is built around Cloverdale's 1881 Town Hall. Visitors will also enjoy the brisk antique trade centered in Cloverdale.

Ladner, Tsawwassen, Delta

Delta was founded in 1868, by William and Thomas Ladner, two brothers rich from the gold mines in Lillooet, who decided to try their hand at farming. Located between the south arm of the Fraser River and Boundary Bay, Delta is still a rich agricultural region. Since the opening of the George Massey Tunnel in 1959, however, Delta has become a convenient home for commuters and neighbourhoods have sprung up where farms once were. With the new development has come a new urban sensibility, reflected in retail centers like Delta Village.

Chinatown

The first Chinese immigrants arrived in British Columbia in the 1850s. After helping to blast the national railway through the mountains of western Canada, many settled in Vancouver along Pender Street. Here they created a world reminiscent of the home they had left in Canton. Businessmen erected buildings reflecting a distinct architecture of recessed balconies enclosed by elaborate wrought iron and decorated cornices. The largely male working class lived in the narrow, wooden tenement buildings still visible on Pender today. By day they would leave home to work as houseboys, launderers, cooks and mill workers. In the evening they would gather and socialize in the streets and restaurants, or in the gambling rooms and baths that were hidden underground, and along the back alleys. However, those of Chinese heritage have greatly spread out and diversified today. Richmond has developed the busy, modern day flavour of a Little Kong Kong and also boasts a beautiful buddhist temple. The city's old Chinatown preserves the distinctive character and culture of Vancouver's original Chinese immigrants. It remains a bustling , vital market district where savvy shoppers jostle along streets overflowing with Asian speciality groceries, houseware shops and herbalists. Restaurants here still serve up the traditional delicacies of Canton.

Iona Park

Iona Beach Regional Park, located on Iona Island, in the North Arm of Fraser River, is a great location for short sight-seeing day trips. A four kilometer walk down the spit provides views of the Vancouver International Airport, river traffic, and the occasional Bald Eagle feeding on fish near the shore. At dusk, people wait to see some of the most beautiful sunsets over the Strait of Georgia that Vancouver has to offer, as seen in our main photograph. In the lower photo is a view of a part of the airport's new terminal building and a photograph of Fantasy Gardens, located in Richmond.

Steveston

Part of Richmond, the historic village of Steveston is a picturesque fishing community, nestled along the Fraser River on the south side of Lulu Island. Founded in 1889 by William Steeves, Steveston had more than a dozen fish canneries by the 1890's and supported hotels, saloons and an opera house. Japanese immigrants played a large part in Steveston's prosperity, bringing fishing expertise, staffing canneries, and founding Richmond's first hospital. A good place to learn about Steveston's interesting history is the Steveston Museum, housed in a building erected in 1950. Today Steveston is a prime location for commuters looking for a peaceful place to live outside the city. It is also a prime tourist attraction with its pretty shops, delicious seafood and panoramic views of the ocean. Heritage buildings abound in Steveston are easily seen during a short walking tour of the town. Through the Steveston Public Market is the Steveston Wharf, which remains the heart of this pretty village. Here, cluttered and colourful fishing boats crowd the dock that fronts the fishing harbour. Shoppers are drawn all the way from Vancouver for the fresh fish sold out of their holds. On Canada Day, July 1st, everyone can enjoy a taste of Steveston at the celebratory Salmon Festival's salmon bake-off.

Richmond

Richmond is a collection of islands in the delta formed by the north and south arms of the Fraser River. On average, Richmond is less than two metres above sea level, and in many spots, below the sea. An interconnecting system of dikes keeps the ocean out, but they also serve as popular walking, jogging and cycling paths. Just across the Arthur Laing Bridge from Vancouver to Sea Island is the Vancouver International Airport. Taking off and landing right over the ocean can be quite a spectacular way to glimpse Vancouver's natural beauty. The flat landscape makes it easy to see a windmill by the side of Highway 99, just before the Steveston Interchange. This landmark is just one of the dutch influenced attractions at Fantasy Gardens, a colourful show garden and religious theme park. The rich, silty earth of Richmond has historically provided rich land for horticulture and agriculture, but Richmond is developing quickly as a secondary urban centre to Vancouver. Richmond's population boom is due in large part to a growing Asian Community largely from Hong Kong. A visit to the serene Buddhist Temple and the bustling Aberdeen Mall, or to the Yaohan Centre will reveal the contrasts of this vital community.

Coquitlam

Coquitlam and Port Coquitlam are two sprawling suburbs east of Vancouver that stretch from the north side of the Fraser River to the shores of Burrard Inlet around the base of Coquitlam Mountain. Coquitlam was incorporated as a municipality in 1891. Later, in 1913, Port Coquitlam seceded from Coquitlam to form its own municipality. The area developed very slowly for the first half of the century. Primarily a logging area, Coquitlam and Port Coquitlam concentrated on developing an industrial base around huge enterprises like the Fraser Mills. When the Lougheed Highway was completed in the 1950's, the region became easily accessible from Vancouver, and vast tracts of suburban housing sprang up. The pace of development has sped the urbanization of both areas. Outside their busy commercial centers, however, many peaceful natural spots remain. Minnekhana Regional Park is a lovely spot for picnics and walks with a historic lodge and a marsh rich with wildlife. Mundy Park provides 435 acres of dense forest for wilderness adventuring. The PoCo Trail winds along 29 kilometres of the Coquitlam, and Pitt River and offers scenic walking, cycling and horseback riding. Photograph at left shows Buntzen Lake in Belcarra Regional Park.

Pitt Meadows

East of Vancouver, just across the Pitt River, is Pitt Meadows, a fertile agricultural lowland between the slopes of Port Coquitlam and the forested hills of Maple Ridge. Pitt Meadows is still largely rural with a patch-work of berry fields and dairy farms covering its vast fields. The dikes along the Pitt River offer easy, flat strolls. The waters of Pitt Lake and Pitt River are both peaceful recreation spots popular with canoeists. Maple Ridge is similarly rural, but instead of berry-picking, here the visitor is likely to saddle up and take off horse-back riding. With a host of stables and riding schools, Maple Ridge is known as the horse capital of Canada. The rolling, wooded pastures of Maple Ridge support over 160 kilometres of riding trails. Located in Maple Ridge are the vast, forested mountains of Golden Ears Provincial Park, one of the largest camping areas in British Columbia with some 350 campsites. Although they remain largely rural, these pastoral havens outside Vancouver are beginning to feel the pressure of urban growth, as more and more people choose a long commute and suburban calm over crowds and expensive housing.

Fraser River, Delta

Despite sprawling growth, Fraser River Delta remains a naturalist's dream and a bird watcher's paradise. Burns Bog, a huge expanse of undeveloped wetland between North Delta and Ladner, attracts hundreds of wintering birds each year. The protected cove at Boundary Bay is reported to have Canada's largest wintertime population of hawks, eagles, and falcons. The most popular spot for bird watching in Delta is the Reifel Bird Sanctuary. At 340 hectares (839 acres,) it's a small remnant of the estuary marshes that once covered much of the Fraser River Delta. Located on the North American Pacific migratory flyway, the sanctuary attracts thousands of birds with some 250 species represented—from the common Canada goose, to the rare spotted redshank. (The photographs at this page: Aerial view of the delta of Fraser River, Queensborough and the Annacis Island with the Alex Fraser Bridge.)

Fraser Valley

The Fraser Valley is a greenbelt of berry fields, farmlands, pastures, and pleasant towns east of the urban sprawl of Greater Vancouver. Most of the fresh produce city dwellers enjoy all year long, and the fruit they enjoy in the warmer months is grown in the rich, silty earth of the Fraser Valley. In the summer, vacationers travel through this flat delta along the Trans-Canada Highway on their way up to the scenic Coquihalla Highway, leading to the horse ranches of Merritt, the arid lakefronts of the Okanagan, and the lofty peaks of the Rocky Mountains. The popular holiday spots of Harrison Hot Springs and Cultus Lake are nestled in the Fraser Valley. Along with the farms of the valley are several prime attractions. The most popular is the Abbotsford International Airshow, held every August. Considered the leading airshow in North America, this event draws more than 100,000 spectators each day to its breathtaking flights and fascinating displays. (The photographs on this page are of Maple Ridge by the Fraser River and a general view of the Fraser Valley from Cypress.)

Inside Passage Gate

Vancouver Harbour is the gate to the famous Inside Passage. The way through the Inside Passage became very popular with cruise trips in the early 1950's. Today, numerous luxury cruise ships—some with over 2,000 passengers—leave Vancouver Harbour several times weekly in summer months to their journeys through Strait of Georgia and Hecate Strait into the Gulf of Alaska, around British Columbia's shores and Alaska's islands. They stop in the Alaskan ports of Sitka, Ketchikan, Juneau, Skagway and Haines, passing by Columbia and Hubbard Glaciers, and through Prince Edward Sound to the last stop at the port of Seward. An amazing trip for those who want to see Alaska from the sea and visit several ports for a day to see attractions around the areas. *(For more photographs from the Inside Passage, Alaska and Yukon, please refer to our Alaska-Yukon book.)*